NANCY WAKE

The White Mouse Who
Defied the Nazis

Written By:

Jameson Maxwell

Copyright © 2024 Jameson Maxwell
Alright Reversed.
No part of this biography may be reproduced, distributed, or transmitted in any form or by any means, including photocopying, recording, or other electronic or mechanical methods, without the prior written permission of the copyright holder, except in the case of brief quotations embodied in critical reviews and certain other noncommercial uses permitted by copyright law.

Table Of Contents

Introduction
Chapter 1　Early Life and Family Background
Chapter 2　The World Beyond
Chapter 3　The War Begins
Chapter 4　Joining the Resistance
Chapter 5　The White Mouse
Chapter 6　Betrayal and Escape
Chapter 7　The Special Operations Executive
Chapter 8　Liberation and Loss
Chapter 9　Aftermath and Recognition
Chapter 10　Legacy of a Hero
Conclusion
Bonus　50 moral quotes inspired by Nancy Wake's biography

Introduction

In the murky world of resistance and espionage, where bravery is needed and betrayal is essential, one woman became renowned. Nancy Wake, a symbol of defiance against repressive dictatorships, earned the nickname "The White Mouse" from the Gestapo for her amazing ability to evade capture. This is the story of a lady whose unwavering quest for independence altered the direction of the conflict.

Imagine a vibrant, attractive young woman who, abandoning the comforts of her previous life, fled the underground of occupied France in favor of the protection of Parisian high society. She spent her days mingling with the elite and her nights organizing guerrilla attacks against the Nazis, planning acts of sabotage and rescuing downed pilots. Nancy Wake embodied every horrifying escape and defiance you might anticipate from a spy story.

Having come from humble beginnings in Australia and New Zealand, Wake's remarkable perseverance is shown by her status as one of the most decorated women of World War II. She was one of the most resilient people in history; she overcame fear, negotiated a culture where male resistance fighters predominated, and battled unceasingly for a cause greater than herself.

This in-depth biography of Elizabeth Wake explores her dual persona and how she developed from a reckless socialite to a determined opposition figure. It examines the sacrifices she made for other people, the love she lost, and the influence she had. "Nancy Wake: The White Mouse Who Defied the Nazis" vividly recounts the exploits of a woman who rose to become a symbol of resistance against persecution via meticulous research and engrossing narrative.

As you turn the pages, be ready to enter a world where danger lurks around every corner, trust is hard to come by, and one woman's unwavering spirit has a lasting influence on the path of history. The tale of Nancy Wake serves as a potent reminder of the impact that a single individual may have in the fight for liberty and justice. This is the story of a hero whose legacy inspires generations even now, not just a war story.

Chapter 1

Early Life and Family Background

On August 30, 1912, Nancy Grace Augusta Wake was born in Wellington, New Zealand. She came from a family of six children, the youngest of whom would soon experience instability. Ella Rosieur Wake was a French-born housewife, and her father, Charles Augustus Wake, was a journalist. Nancy's life would later be significantly impacted by this past, which connected her destiny to that of her mother's homeland.

The family moved to Sydney, Australia, shortly after Nancy was born, and there her father deserted them, leaving Ella to raise the kids by herself. Little Nancy was deeply affected by this act of abandoning, which gave her a strong sense of independence and persistence. Ella was determined to support her family despite her financial difficulties, instilling in her kids the values of perseverance and independence.

Family Effects on Early Education

Nancy's childhood in the bustling Sydney suburbs was marked by both adversity and adventure. Nancy found a freedom that rivaled her mother's strict discipline when she explored her local streets and beaches. She developed a bold and audacious attitude as a result of this contrast between freedom and rigidity.

Nancy studied traditional academics and practical skills at the North Sydney Household Arts School. But she often found herself at odds with the conventional expectations of her upbringing due to her restlessness and desire for adventure. She had a gift for embellishing tales of her exploits and was a natural storyteller. These traits would come in handy for her clandestine activities.

Wanderlust & Adventure Dreams

Nancy had always imagined herself outside the confines of her everyday life. She was drawn to tales of exotic places and strange encounters. She saved every penny for her ideal getaway before leaving home at the age of sixteen to work as a nurse. Her hard work paid off when, at the age of 20, she got a little amount of money from an aunt, which enabled her to take the long-awaited trip to Europe.

When Nancy first arrived in London in the early 1930s, she was captivated by the vibrancy and promise of the city. She was able to satisfy her curiosity and hone her observational and communication skills by landing a job as a journalist. Due to her job, she traveled around Europe and was exposed to the political unrest that was about to envelop the continent.

Nancy initially learned the horrible reality of Nazism around this time. Her 1933 reporting trip to Vienna had a lasting impression on her. After she saw firsthand the cruelty and persecution Nazi thugs inflicted upon Jews and political dissidents, Nancy's resolve to oppose such despotism began to take shape.

Bits of Disobedience

Nancy began to see the extent of the threat posed by Adolf Hitler and his regime as she traveled throughout Europe. Her time in Germany and Austria set the groundwork for her subsequent endeavors and sparked a fierce opposition to Nazism. The contrast between her spirit of adventure and the somber reality of a world rapidly approaching conflict gave rise to a sense of purpose that would guide her actions in the years that followed.

The early years of Nancy Wake's life were a prelude to a life marked by courage and defiance. The girl who wandered the streets of London and the beaches of Sydney would soon rise to prominence in the struggle against one of the worst dictatorships in history. These formative experiences transformed her from a disobedient child into a terrifying leader known as "The White Mouse."

Chapter 2

The World Beyond

Young People with Adventure
Nancy Wake set off on a journey that would take her far from Australia's coastlines and into the tumultuous heart of Europe, leaving behind the comforts of Sydney. When she first arrived in London in the early 1930s, she was captivated by the dynamic energy and seemingly endless opportunities of the city. Here, among the bustling streets and historic landmarks,

Nancy's appetite for adventure began to really take hold.

Nancy Relocating to Europe

Nancy first came into contact with the outside world in London. She quickly secured a job as a journalist with her usual tenacity and resourcefulness, keen to learn about the complex web of European politics and culture. Her work took her all across the continent, from the bustling streets of Paris to the picturesque villages of the Swiss Alps.

London and Parisian lifestyles

Nancy thrived in the fast-paced world of journalism in London. She was well-known in the industry for her sharp wit and keen intellect, but she was also quite charming to both friends and coworkers. Nancy, however, was really enthralled with the city of lights and passion—Paris. Absorbing herself in the vibrant nightlife and cutting-edge culture of the city, she relished the liberty and excitement that Paris had to offer.

Early Journalistic Career

Nancy had a front-row seat to the events that would soon engulf Europe in war as a journalist, covering everything from social gatherings to political protests. She developed a reputation as a perceptive and sympathetic reporter because of her ability to capture the essence of each story via her keen eye for detail and knack for storytelling. However, underneath the polish of her work was a growing unease. Nancy's journalistic instincts drove her to delve further into the political unrest engulfing the continent as the threat of fascism loomed larger on the horizon. It was a decision that would permanently alter her course and lead her down a dangerous and intriguing path.

Nancy Wake, standing on the cusp of history, could never have imagined the role she would play in was well-known in the industry for her sharp wit and keen intellect, but she was also quite charming to both friends and coworkers. Nancy, however, was really enthralled with the city of lights and passion—Paris. Absorbing herself in the vibrant nightlife and cutting-edge culture of the city, she relished the liberty and excitement that Paris had to offer.

Early Journalistic Career

Nancy had a front-row seat to the events that would soon engulf Europe in war as a journalist, covering everything from social gatherings to political protests. She developed a reputation as a perceptive and sympathetic reporter because of her ability to capture the essence of each story via her keen eye for detail and knack for storytelling. However, underneath the polish of her work was a growing unease. Nancy's journalistic instincts drove her to delve further into the political unrest engulfing the continent as the threat of fascism loomed larger on the horizon. It was a decision that would permanently alter her course and lead her down a dangerous and intriguing path.

Nancy Wake, standing on the cusp of history, could never have imagined the role she would play in shaping nations' futures. She would, however, prove to be a formidable force as the world plunged into conflict—a woman willing to reject authority and stand up to the powers that be. Nancy set off to explore the world beyond, prepared to face any challenges that lay ahead, with the winds of destiny at her back.

Chapter 3

The War Begins

Observing the Fascist Rise
Nancy Wake found herself in the midst of a continent consumed by fear and uncertainty as Europe teetered on the brink of war. Reporting from the front lines of history, she saw directly the dark shadow cast over the world by fascism and its unstoppable rise to power. She saw the seeds of the violence that would soon engulf the world sprouting from the roots of

tyranny and hatred in the streets of Vienna and the beer halls of Berlin.

Reporting on Nazism's Ascent

Nancy's natural curiosity drove her to delve further into the heart of the evil that was engulfing Europe. She started on a series of audacious investigations that exposed the brutality of the Nazi regime because she had a keen eye for detail and a fearless desire to find the truth. Nancy's reporting exposed Hitler's henchmen's atrocities, from the persecution of Jews to the suppression of political opposition, which infuriated the Nazi leadership.

Berlin and Vienna experiences

Nancy arrived in Vienna, a city on the verge of collapse, during the winter of 1933. She saw the cunning methods used by the Nazis to manipulate and control the populace amid the whirling clouds of propaganda and misinformation. She would be plagued by this awful realization of the oppressive system for years to come.

Berlin, the throbbing hub of the Nazi empire, was the destination of her next journey. Here, Nancy saw the true face of fascism amid the opulence of the Reichstag and the terrifying Gestapo. The sound of propaganda and the thud of jackboots filled the streets as Hitler's minions worked ruthlessly to crush any opposition. But despite all of the chaos and sadness, Nancy's determination to resist the forces of evil simply became stronger.

The Choice to Enter the Battle

With war imminent, Nancy had to decide whether to use force to combat the oppressive powers or to remain silent while chaos descended over the planet. Nancy found the choice to be simple. She knew full well the risks involved, yet she made the decision to join the fight against fascism with a steely resolve of conviction and courage. So, with her arms raised to face whatever was ahead, Nancy Wake went bravely into the battlefield as storm clouds gathered and the sounds of war reverberated over the continent.

Chapter 4

Joining the Resistance

Journalist to Spy and Back Again

One of Nancy Wake's most significant life turning points was her transition from an adventurous journalist to a fearless resistance fighter. She tragically decided to join the French Resistance in response to the prospect of Nazism taking over Europe, prepared to do whatever it took to prevent the Nazis from taking over her cherished adopted country.

Early Participation in the French Resistance

Nancy arrived in France with a strong sense of purpose and dedication, and she quickly immersed herself in the resistance's covert society. She quickly became well-liked by significant figures in the underground network by using her natural charm and journalistic skills, winning their respect and trust. From safe houses to covert rendezvous locations, Nancy moved deftly through the shadowy corridors of the resistance, gathering intelligence and carrying out covert operations with precision and competence.

Instruction and Initial Missions

As her commitment to the resistance grew, Nancy underwent extensive training in guerilla warfare, espionage, and sabotage techniques. She honed her skills in handling weapons, deciphering codes, and secret communication under the watchful eye of seasoned operators, readying herself for the lethal missions that lay ahead.

Her first missions were a baptism by fire, putting her will and tenacity to the test in the face of significant challenges. Nancy showed herself to be a fearless and competent spy, willing to give up everything for the cause of freedom, by scuttling vital supply lines and smuggling Allied pilots to safety behind enemy lines.

Wedlock to Henri Fiocca and Their Secret Activities

Nancy first made the acquaintance of the stunning and energetic Frenchman, Henri Fiocca, at this time. He would go on to become her partner in both love and war. Nancy and Henri embarked on a number of dangerous missions together, bound by their shared commitment to the resistance. Their love for one another served as a ray of hope at their most hopeless moments.

Together, they planned a sabotage and disinformation operation that made the Nazi invaders fearful. Nancy and Henri gained a reputation as two of the most formidable figures in the resistance by using their skill and delicacy to assault targets such as railroad lines and German patrols.

However, their happiness was fleeting, because the dreadful hand of war soon reached out to tear them apart. Nancy was left feeling abandoned and distressed when Henri was apprehended by the

Gestapo in the summer of 1943 and executed. Nevertheless, Nancy vowed to go on with the fight in his memory even in the depths of her grief.

Nancy Wake's name became connected with bravery, tenacity, and resistance as her reputation grew. For Nancy, however, the true test of her success lay not in accolades or recognition but rather in the realization that she had done all within her power to oppose oppression and injustice. Thus, Nancy Wake remained unwavering in her commitment to the cause of freedom while fighting on the front lines of history, providing hope in a world destroyed by tyranny.

Chapter 5

The White Mouse

Avoidance and Deceit

Nancy Wake's transformation into "The White Mouse" was a tribute to her cunning as well as an example of her unwavering determination. Nancy's ability to avoid capture grew legendary as the Gestapo tightened its grip on occupied France, earning her a reputation as one of the resistance's most elusive figures.

Nancy often avoided capture by outwitting the Nazi authorities with a combination of quick thinking and steely grit. She moved unnoticed through the streets of Paris, gathering intelligence and deftly organizing sabotage operations while disguising herself as a washerwoman, a nun, or a beggar.

But Nancy's nickname, "The White Mouse," did not come from her ability to avoid capture. Her exceptional ability to instill fear in her opponents and leave them confused and agitated by her evasiveness was another. She seemed to vanish into thin air, like a ghost in the night, leaving only whispers and tales of her presence.

Getting Known as "The White Mouse"

There is controversy and uncertainty around the origins of Nancy's nickname. Some others think the Gestapo itself, frustrated by her repeated ability to elude them, were the ones who devised it. Some people think that other resistance fighters gave it to her because they respected her bravery and resourcefulness in the face of danger. Whatever its origins, the nickname stuck around and came to represent Nancy's obstinacy and tenacity in the face of overwhelming challenges. She was more than just a resistance fighter to the people of occupied France; to them, she represented hope and courage in an otherwise dismal world.

Avoiding the Gestapo's Trap

Though the Gestapo pursued her relentlessly, Nancy managed to stay one step ahead of her potential abductors. She repeatedly eluded their grasp by using her cunning and intelligence to outsmart them at every turn. Nancy was always able to avoid being arrested, whether it was by hiding in plain sight or by sliding through the cracks in their surveillance, leaving her pursuers bewildered and disappointed in her wake.

But the stakes were higher than ever for Nancy. Countless resistance fighters looked to her for support, so she knew that failure was not an option. Every mission, every escape, meant the difference between life and death, not just for her, but also for the many others who looked up to her as an inspiration and leader.

Important Tasks and Countermeasures

Nancy Wake, also known as "The White Mouse," was a key player in some of the most audacious and daring acts of the French Resistance. She instilled fear in the minds of the Nazi invaders by blowing up enemy supply depots and ambushing German patrols, leaving a trail of destruction in her wake.

But Nancy's influence extended beyond her skill as a saboteur; it also stemmed from her capacity to inspire others to take up the fight against despotism. She inspired her fellow resistance fighters to take up arms against injustice with her infectious passion and unwavering dedication to the cause, showing them that hope could always triumph over despair even in the most dire circumstances.

Nancy Wake's desire to bring the Nazi administration to its fall grew along with her notoriety. She moved one step closer to realizing her ultimate goal of liberating France and overthrowing Nazism with each mission and narrow escape. Even while Nancy understood that victory would eventually be within reach, she also realized that the path ahead would be difficult and dangerous.

Chapter 6

Betrayal and Escape

The Gestapo Draws Near

Nancy Wake's renown increased along with the Gestapo's determination to apprehend her. She turned into a thorn in the side of the Nazi invaders with every risky trip and narrow escape, inspiring fear in their hearts with her courage and resourcefulness. But Nancy soon discovered that her good fortune could only last so long as the net grew tighter around her.

Nancy's Escape and Henri Fiocca's Capture

Tragedy occurred in the summer of 1943 when Henri Fiocca, Nancy's devoted husband, was taken prisoner by the Gestapo. Nancy was devastated by the loss and determined to take all necessary steps to get his release. However, tragedy struck again when she embarked on a risky rescue mission and discovered that Henri had been slain by his captors, leaving her devastated and alone.

As the Gestapo closed in on her location, Nancy knew she had to act quickly to avoid being taken into custody. She managed to evade her assailants and escape into the French countryside with the help of other resistance fighters, resolved to carry on the fight in Henri's memory.

Difficult Travel to Spain

Nancy, having to face the harsh reality of life on the run, took a dangerous journey over the Pyrenees Mountains in an attempt to reach neutral Spain. She narrowly avoided being apprehended by German patrols and complicit French officials by using her cunning and intelligence to manoeuvre across the treacherous terrain, where danger lurked around every corner.

Nancy struggled for days against fatigue, hunger, and the constant threat of being discovered as she travelled in the direction of the safety of the Spanish border. She was confronted with the greatest challenge of her life, but instead of letting it break her, she found strength in the memory of Henri and the many others who had perished in the struggle against Nazism.

Entry into the United Kingdom

Following weeks of hardship and uncertainty, Nancy eventually made it to the safety of British territory, where she was welcomed as a hero and a symbol of defiance against oppression. Nancy was determined to bring the Nazi system to its knees even if she had lost a lot along the way.

Nancy knew the fight was far from over as she looked out over the coasts of her chosen country. Her heart burning with the memory of Henri, she resolved to fight fascism until its last vestiges were destroyed and a world free of oppression and tyranny was left in its wake. And despite the long and perilous road ahead, Nancy Wake never wavered in her commitment to the cause of freedom, serving as a ray of hope in a world where darkness reigned.

Chapter 7

The Special Operations Executive

Go Back to Fighting

Nancy Wake's courage never wavered in the face of threats and the tragic loss of her spouse. She seized the opportunity to join the Special Activities Executive (SOE), a secret organisation tasked with carrying out sabotage and espionage activities behind enemy lines, since she was determined to keep fighting the Nazi occupation of France.

Getting trained in Britain with the SOE

Nancy had extensive training with the SOE in Britain, honing her skills in sabotage operations, secret communication, and weapon handling. She learned the craft of deception and stealth under the watchful eyes of seasoned operatives, readying herself for the lethal missions that were ahead.

Returning to France by parachute

Nancy returned to France as a full-fledged agent of the SOE, prepared to carry out her role in the resistance, armed with the knowledge and skills she had acquired throughout her training. Under the cover of darkness, she made her way into enemy territory and began a series of risky actions aimed at weakening the Nazi occupation and bolstering the morale of the French people.

Leading the Maquis in Guerrilla Warfare

Nancy was an essential figure in the planning of sabotage operations and ambushes against German patrols as a leader of the Maquis, the French resistance fighters who waged guerilla warfare against the Nazi invaders. She established herself as a formidable foe of the Nazi regime thanks to her in-depth familiarity of the French countryside and her capacity to inspire others to join the resistance.

The Concluding Missions and the French Liberation

Nancy took part in some of the most audacious acts of the French resistance during the last stages of the war, such as the liberation of Toulouse. She organised the last assault against the Nazi invaders with the assistance of Allied forces, paving the way for the liberation of France and the fall of Nazism in Europe.

Thoughts on the Price of War

Nancy Wake assessed the enormous sacrifices made in the fight against despotism when the guns stopped firing and the dust fell on the European front lines. Even though she had suffered much personally as a result of the fighting, she knew that the struggle for freedom was far from over.

Nancy, her heart heavy with grief for her fallen friends, made up her mind to honour their sacrifice by dedicating herself to the work of peace and reconciliation. She was hopeful that one day the world would learn from its mistakes and work to create a future free from the horrors of violence, even if the wounds caused by war would never fully heal.

Nancy Wake realised she had been a part of something very unique as she reflected on her time with the SOE. She had been able to change the course of history by her courage, dedication, and sacrifice; she had been instrumental in the downfall of one of the worst crimes the world had ever seen. Despite the dangers and hardships that accompanied her journey, she came out of the shadows stronger and more determined than ever to fight for a better future.

Chapter 8

Liberation and Loss

The Concluding Missions and the French Liberation

Nancy Wake persisted in her unrelenting battle against the Nazi invaders as the Allied troops pushed forward throughout Europe, taking part in a number of audacious operations meant to speed up the liberation of France. She defeated the forces of oppression with every operation, inspiring her fellow resistance fighters to persevere in the face of insurmountable obstacles.

Paris's Liberation

Nancy's efforts were rewarded in August 1944 when Paris revolted against the German invaders. She joined the ranks of the French resistance fighters who heroically battled to rescue their beloved city from the grip of tyranny as the streets resonated with the sound of gunfire and the screams of liberty.

Nancy saw the liberation of Paris as a sign of the human spirit's tenacity and will, as well as a moment of victory and validation. She was overcome with pride at what she and the other resistance fighters had done as she stood among the debris and wreckage of the city she had battled so valiantly to free.

The Heart-wrenching News of Henri Fiocca's Death

However, tragedy came during the triumphant celebrations when Nancy learned that her husband Henri Fiocca died by the Gestapo. Nancy was dealt a devastating blow when Henri passed away, and it would take her a long time to get out of her sorrow and misery.

Thoughts on the Price of War

Nancy Wake struggled to comprehend the magnitude of the sacrifices made as the war came to an end and the globe started to rebuild after the battle. The devastation of cities, the death toll, and the bereaved loved ones all served as sobering reminders of the human cost of war.

Nancy, however, held onto hope that the lessons learned from the past would not be lost despite the anguish and suffering. She committed herself to working for peace and reconciliation in order to pay tribute to the memories of those who had died. Even though the wounds from the conflict would never completely heal, she never wavered in her conviction that a better world was achievable.

A Legacy of Bravery and Tenacity

Nancy Wake realised she had been a part of something genuinely exceptional when she reflected on her experiences throughout the war. She had shaped history by her bravery, tenacity, and sacrifice; she was instrumental in the abolition of one of the worst atrocities the world had ever known.

Nancy came out of the darkness stronger and more motivated than ever to fight for a brighter future, despite the fact that the journey had been long and dangerous. Even though she would always carry the memories of the battle with her, she was aware that the legacy of bravery and resiliency created during those difficult times would last for many generations.

Chapter 9

Aftermath and Recognition

Life After the War

Nancy Wake was confronted with the difficult undertaking of reconstructing her life after the war. Despite her profound wounds from the war, she refused to let the horrors of the past define her and instead focused her hope and drive on the future.

After years spent in the furnace of battle, Nancy found it difficult to acclimate to the relative calm of peacetime upon her return to civilian life. Nevertheless, she never wavered in her will to change the world and to carry on the struggle for freedom and justice in spite of the difficulties she encountered.

Getting Used to Peacetime

Nancy had mixed emotions as she adjusted to peacetime. Moments of joy and pleasure came from reuniting with loved ones who had survived the war, but her newfound independence was clouded by their absence.

Nancy took comfort in the idea that her friends' and allies' efforts had not been in vain, despite her sadness at their passing. By securing a future free from tyranny, their courage and tenacity had laid the groundwork for a society where the values of freedom and peace might thrive.

Appreciation and Praise

Nancy Wake's extraordinary courage and valour started to get public notice and praise in the years after the war. She was recognized for her services to the Allied cause and was given many honours and decorations, including the American Medal of Freedom and the British George Medal.

However, Nancy believed that the real test of her achievement was not the recognition she got but rather the awareness that she had improved the lives of others. She was aware that every brave deed, whether it was scuttling Allied troops from behind enemy lines or organising risky sabotage operations against the Nazi invaders, had tipped the odds in favour of justice and freedom.

Composing Her Memoir and Giving Public Talks

Following the war, Nancy Wake wrote a book titled "The White Mouse," which captured the attention of readers worldwide with its inspiring stories of bravery, tenacity, and resistance in the face of insurmountable circumstances. The narrative detailed her remarkable experiences throughout the war. She aimed to encourage future generations to resist tyranny and injustice by reminding them that one person can make a difference even in the most difficult circumstances via her writing.

Nancy gained popularity as a writer and public speaker, sharing her experiences with listeners all around the world. She travelled the world, speaking to civic groups, schools, and veterans' organisations as well as any open ears, sharing her message of hope and perseverance.

Sustaining Motivation for Opposition to Tyranny

Nancy Wake realised that her legacy would live on long after her passing as she reflected on her extraordinary life. She had led a life marked by bravery, tenacity, and a fiery devotion to freedom, from her modest origins in Australia and New Zealand to her daring adventures in occupied France.

Even though a lot had happened in the decades after the war ended, Nancy continued to be a symbol of defiance against injustice and tyranny, encouraging countless others to strive for a better future and stand up for what they believed in. Even though she had encountered several difficulties along the road, she was aware that each one had only served to strengthen her determination and confirm her faith in the ability of the human spirit to triumph over the most formidable barriers.

Chapter 10

Legacy of a Hero

Durable Effect

Beyond space and time, Nancy Wake's heroism from World War II transcends all limits. Her steadfast tenacity, unselfish commitment to the cause of freedom, and indomitable spirit have made a lasting impression on history. More than that, however, her legacy endures in the thoughts and feelings of those who are still moved by her remarkable life.

Nancy Wake's Contribution to the War Mission

Nancy Wake made outstanding contributions to the Allied cause during the war. She was instrumental in the fall of the Nazi dictatorship and the liberation of Europe, both via her fearless operations conducted behind enemy lines and her leadership in the French Resistance.

Her example for the next generation is possibly her greatest legacy, however. Nancy demonstrated that women were just as capable of courage and heroism as men were at a time when males ruled society.

Stereotypes were dispelled and a new generation of female activists and leaders was made possible by her gutsy resistance in the face of insurmountable difficulties.

Impact on Next Generations

The impact of Nancy Wake goes well beyond what happened during her lifetime. Many people all throughout the globe, from future activists and resistance fighters to historians and academics, are still motivated by her narrative. Her extraordinary life has been preserved for future generations to learn from and appreciate via books, movies, and documentaries.

However, her influence on those who knew her directly may be her greatest legacy. She was a dependable comrade and a strong leader to her fellow resistance soldiers. She represented hope and rebellion against injustice to the people of France. In sad times, she also provided support and inspiration to her friends and loved ones.

Last Years and Dying

Nancy Wake had a modest life in her latter years, away from the limelight and publicity surrounding her wartime adventures. Nevertheless, she never wavered in her dedication to the principles she cherished—freedom, justice, and equality for all—even as she grew older.

Nancy Wake, who was 98 years old, died quietly in her sleep in August 2011 and left behind a legacy that will last for many generations. Despite her passing, her legacy endures in the hearts of those who knew her and in the many lives she touched with her bravery and generosity.

Recalling Nancy Wake

As time goes on and the memories of World War II disappear, Nancy Wake's influence endures and becomes stronger than ever. She was the epitome of bravery and selflessness, from her modest upbringing in Australia and New Zealand to her fearless actions in occupied France.

Her name is now linked to bravery, tenacity, and resistance to oppression. Whether in the poignant words of remembrance or the silent times of contemplation, Nancy Wake's legacy shines brightly and inspires everyone who aspires to improve the world. Even though she is no longer with us, her memory endures via the heroic legacy of a brave person who dared to envision a society in which freedom is paramount.

Conclusion

Nancy Wake's name is immortalised in history as a brave and defiant woman who stood up against oppression. Her incredible transformation from a carefree young lady to one of the most honoured heroines of World War II is proof of the human spirit's ability to triumph over the most difficult obstacles.

Despite suffering and making sacrifices throughout her life, Nancy remained steadfast in her support of the liberation movement. She left behind a legacy that will last for many decades by influencing the course of history with her courage, resiliency, and unflinching drive.

More than anything, however, Nancy Wake's legacy acts as a reminder of the immense potential for good that each and every one of us has. Her tale gives us hope in a world when disagreement and war are commonplace, demonstrating that one individual can make a difference even in the most difficult circumstances.

As we consider Nancy's extraordinary life and contributions, let us remember her by carrying on the struggle for freedom, equality, and justice for everyone. As we work to create a society that upholds and celebrates the principles she held dear—courage, compassion, and integrity—let us be inspired by her example.

Nancy Wake may be no longer with us, but her memory endures in the hearts of those who knew her and the many lives she impacted. And the legacy of a hero who dared to dream of a better world and who, by her deeds, helped to make that goal a reality, will live on as long as her memory does.

Bonus

50 moral quotes inspired by Nancy Wake's biography:

1. "Courage is not the absence of fear, but the triumph over it."
2. "In the face of tyranny, resilience is a form of defiance."
3. "One person's bravery can inspire a movement."
4. "True heroism is about fighting for justice, no matter the cost."
5. "Standing up to evil requires both strength and resolve."
6. "Even in the darkest times, hope can light the way."

7. "Self-sacrifice is the highest form of patriotism."

8. "Resistance against oppression is a moral duty."

9. "The spirit of freedom cannot be crushed by fear."

10. "Every act of courage chips away at tyranny."

11. "The fight for freedom is a fight for humanity."

12. "Never underestimate the power of a determined individual."

13. "Adversity reveals the true character of a person."

14. "The strength of the human spirit is boundless."

15. "Injustice anywhere is a threat to justice everywhere."

16. "A true leader inspires others to find their own courage."

17. "Liberty is worth fighting for, even at great personal cost."

18. "Daring to dream of a better world is the first step to achieving it."

19. "Heroes are ordinary people who make extraordinary choices."

20. "The greatest battles are fought with the heart, not just the hands."

21. "Fear is temporary, but freedom is eternal."

22. "The power of one can transform the lives of many."

23. "Hope is the weapon that can never be taken away."

24. "Each act of defiance against tyranny is a victory for justice."

25. "True bravery is standing up for what is right, even when you stand alone."

26. "The legacy of courage inspires generations to come."

27. "Freedom is the birthright of every human being."

28. "Inaction in the face of evil is complicity."

29. "The cost of liberty is eternal vigilance."

30. "Even in loss, there is honor in fighting for what is just."

31. "The pursuit of justice is a lifelong commitment."

32. "One's legacy is built on acts of courage and kindness."

33. "To resist tyranny is to affirm our shared humanity."

34. "History remembers those who fought for the oppressed."

35. "The fight against oppression is a universal struggle."

36. "Courageous acts are the seeds of change."

37. "The spirit of resistance is a beacon of hope."

38. "Strength lies in the willingness to confront fear."

39. "True leaders emerge in times of crisis."

40. "In the struggle for justice, every voice counts."

41. "The greatest battles are fought with integrity and honor."

42. "The courage to fight for others defines true heroism."

43. "Hope and resilience can conquer even the greatest of evils."

44. "The price of freedom is the willingness to fight for it."

45. "Even in despair, there is always a path to hope."

46. "A just cause is worth every sacrifice."

47. "The fight for freedom is a fight for the future."

48. "The courage of one can ignite the spirit of many."

49. "True freedom is achieved through collective action."

50. "The legacy of a hero lives on in the hearts of those they inspire."

These quotes encapsulate the essence of Nancy Wake's life and her unwavering commitment to justice and freedom.

Printed in the USA
CPSIA information can be obtained
at www.ICGtesting.com
LVHW021026241124
797457LV00029B/1109